Your Call Keeps Us Awake

For Ken and Chris

with great affection

Allan

Your Call Keeps Us Awake

Selected Poems of Rocco Scotellaro
Translated by Caroline Maldonado
and Allen Prowle

Published 2013 by
Smokestack Books
PO Box 408, Middlesbrough TS5 6WA
e-mail: info@smokestack-books.co.uk
www.smokestack-books.co.uk

Your Call Keeps Us Awake
Selected Poems of Rocco Scotellaro
Copyright 2004, Arnoldo Mondadori Editore SpA, Milano.
Translations copyright: Caroline Maldonado and Allen Prowle
Cover image: Carlo Levi, Ritratto di Rocco Scotellaro, 1961
(reproduction by Vito Sacco). The private collection of Teresa
and Filomena Mazzarone of Tricarico (Matera), whom we thank
for their kind permission.

Printed and bound in the U.K. by Biddles, part of the
MPG Books Group Ltd, Bodmin & King's Lynn.

ISBN 978-0-9571722-4-1

Middlesbrough
moving forward

Smokestack Books is
represented by Inpress Ltd
www.inpressbooks.co.uk

Al popolo di Tricarico

To the people of Tricarico

Acknowledgements

Acknowledgements are due to *Modern Poetry in Translation (MPT)* for its publication of earlier versions of some of these translations in 'Rocco Scotellaro, poems', which was the first of the *MPT* pamphlet series. We are deeply indebted to David and Helen Constantine, *MPT*'s former editors, for their personal commitment to bringing the poetry of Scotellaro to a wider audience, and for the support and encouragement they have consistently given us in realising this collection. We are most grateful to Carmela Biscaglia, Director of the Centro di Documentazione 'Rocco Scotellaro e la Basilicata del Secondo Dopoguerra', and to Vito Sacco, for their invaluable help and advice over a number of textual and cultural questions which arose during our work on these translations.

CM, AP

Indice

Contents

Introduction

In 1948 in the region of Lucania, present day Basilicata, the eminent writer, Carlo Levi, met a young poet and member of the Italian Socialist Party, Rocco Scotellaro. The occasion was the first election campaign of the new Republic, and it was also the beginning of a precious friendship. In his introduction to the 1963 reissue of *Christ Stopped at Eboli*, Levi described the younger man as 'dear to me above all men'. Tragically, the friendship lasted just five years, as Scotellaro died in 1953 of an undiagnosed heart condition at the age of 30. A year after his friend's death, Levi edited the first published collection of Scotellaro's poetry under the title *È Fatto Giorno* ('It's light now'), which was awarded the prestigious Pellegrino and Viareggio prizes in 1954.

Scotellaro's intense engagement with the cultural and literary life of Italy had begun in the years 1943-44, when he was very young. His work had already received acclaim and critical attention after the publication of poems in a number of provincial and national magazines, notably in the newly founded multi-language journal *Botteghe Oscure*. Through his involvement with these literary journals he was able to establish relationships with such major figures as Giorgio Bassani, Italo Calvino, Cesare Pavese and Eugenio Montale and also to read foreign literature through the first translations that were then being published. He became influenced by the work of Sergei Yesenin, with his poems about his Russian peasant ancestry, as well as by Eliot, Verlaine, Mallarmé, Lorca and Rilke.

With the end of the war had come greater political freedom and an urgent drive for social justice. In the arts too, particularly in the narrative genres of film and prose fiction, there was a new focus on the problems and crises that affected the lives of ordinary people. Scotellaro was one of the few to pioneer a new poetry within this broad movement of neo-realism. The cravenly conformist 'telefoni bianchi' of the 1930s (the white telephone was the perfect metonym of material success and of membership of the club of the socially acceptable) had projected wholesome images of a conservative country rooted in family values and respect for order and authority; country life was seen as benign, provident, morally impeccable and socially harmonious. Scotellaro's Lucania was not Arcadia. His poems depicted a region where people struggled desperately to sustain their families on land which had historically been neglected and badly cultivated, where deforestation and polluted water supplies had contributed to the spread of malaria.

It would be misleading, however, to place his poetry exclusively within the broad movement of neo-realism. For counter-balancing his anger at the plight of the rural poor was his deep love of Lucania; there were its other stories to be told, about an ancestral past whose myths and superstitions had been absorbed into its rituals and psyche. In an early poem, 'Mythology' (1943), he signalled his own rejection of the world-weary self-obsession of the 'crepuscular' poets and the vision of the 'hermetics' of mankind's essential solitude: he ironically capitalised 'Nostalgia' and 'Pain' as the titles of the paintings that he had himself hung in what he calls that 'temple to my life'. His epiphany had been the idea of himself *in* history: on the ground where he stood he saw that 'stones and half-lemons squeezed dry' connected him to the present hardships of his countrymen, while 'the shards of vases of glass/ceramic and terracotta' seemed to demand that he had also 'to face their story'. All of these 'nameless things... possess tongues beyond the human.' Scotellaro determined that he would give voice to the silent tongue both of the present and of the past.

Although his work is rooted in Lucania there are many reasons why it should resonate with the English reader. In a recent talk to an Italian audience in Tricarico, David

Constantine suggested 'It may be, for us, that he has much in common with a central tradition in English poetry, well exemplified in such Romantic writers as Blake and Wordsworth. I am thinking of Blake's advice to poets that they should "Labour well the minute Particulars…" Scotellaro does that. And in so doing, he attends to the real circumstances in which real people live their lives. His poetry is rooted in the here and now; "in the very world", as Wordsworth puts it (in his poem 'French Revolution'), "which is the world/Of all of us, - the place where in the end/We find our happiness, or not at all". The poet, rooted and working in the particular, makes of the material something which is at once true to it and figurative of a truth extending beyond that time and place... we are extended into a life larger than our own.' Then there is that abiding affection in many English readers for writing that reconnects this now largely urban and industrialized country to its rural past. In recent years there has been a strong revival of interest in the poetry of John Clare, with whom Scotellaro can be seen to have had much in common: both lived in places remote from the cultural and political centres of power and at times of acute social change at the heart of which, both in nineteenth-century England and twentieth-century Italy, was the burning issue of the ownership of land; both wrote about the natural cycle of rural life, but without sentimentality, celebrating the strengths and enrichment of community while lamenting their erosion and dissipation. Both were poets of *Dasein*, that condition elaborated by David Constantine of *being there*, of drawing inspiration from locality in order to write poems whose substance and reach are universal.

Rocco Scotellaro was born in Tricarico, some forty miles from Aliano, where Levi had been sent into internal exile by the Fascists in 1936. It's a mountainous region, covering an extensive part of the southern Appenines, and is the least populated in the whole of Southern Italy. During the fifty years before Scotellaro was born, for instance, some fifty thousand Lucanians emigrated, mainly to the United States. His father had gone as a young man to Paterson in

New Jersey, but had been forced to return to Italy, setting up a small business as a shoemaker and struggling to bring up a family of four children. He and his wife made great sacrifices to give the young and obviously gifted Rocco an excellent education. His father persuaded him to board with Capuchin friars, assuring him that if the monastic life did not suit him he could leave whenever he chose. He did acknowledge that the brothers had had a profound influence on his moral development, although later his poems were to express his anti-clericalism. Biblical imagery resonates throughout his work, yet his rage at the church establishment (as well as at the state) for betraying what he considered to be the original Christian values is evident in poems such as 'It's light now' and 'Mass to "the Holy Spirit"'. Nor could he forgive the Church for the part it played in the defeat of the Popular Democratic Front (an electoral alliance of the Communist and Socialist parties) through its active support of the Christian Democrats in the 1948 elections.

The friars had also inspired a love of the classics in him, and he excelled in his study of them. After these early years with the Capuchins he went to schools in Matera, Potenza, Bari, finally graduating in classics, at Trento and he never spent more than two years in any of these schools; a number of his poems express the ambiguous and painful tensions which arose from this constant upheaval, a process which continued when he went to university in Rome as a law student.

The history of this region is one of perpetual invasion, opposition, assimilation. Much of Scotellaro's work reflects his fascination with the rich complexity of ancient and accumulated experience that had contributed to the cultural identity of Lucania, something he explored as if he were reading his family tree (in the last years of his life he was to develop an academic and professional interest in ethnology.) In 'Olympics', he calls the first Greek settlers 'our fathers', and celebrates their youthful joy and energy as they built their settlements along the shores and in the mountains. His pride in these Hellenic origins compounded his distress that his own contemporary world had become so impoverished, having now to beg like 'Homer, that poor man who asked/for a trough of bran at Cumae'. At the time of Islam's expansion to the west, the Saracens captured the fortified Greek citadel of Tricarico, one of the high, strategic centres of Lucania. They remained there over a long period of time, during which they brought to this community their mercantile spirit, artisanship and expertise in farming in arid country; the terraced kitchen-gardens they laid out just beyond the town walls and its gateways are still there today, although sadly a little neglected now. In Naples, the homesick young poet of 'Invective against solitude' remembers how 'at the feet of the houses the Milo,/ a torrent in winter and summer,/waters the fertile kitchen-gardens on the stones.' The districts of the town, still known as the Rabatana and the Saracena, with their fortified gateway and streets disposed in a traditional Arab design, testify to the move from a purely military occupation to a residential and peaceful one. Later, in Turin, another place of enforced exile, he writes of 'my hard Saracen fathers', who had fondled him on their knees before eventually telling him 'to walk now on your own' ('Ticket for Turin'). He expresses his feeling of pride in these Arab roots in other poems such as 'The monotonous singing of the Lucanians' and 'Legend of Love'.

There is a sense in which Scotellaro felt these ancestors to have been traduced: the conquering Greeks become beggars, the once powerful and resourceful Saracens become criminal outsiders. His view of the history of his small town was one of continual tension between the centres of power and the lives of ordinary people who had nothing to give but their labour. The Byzantine citadel, the fortified gateway of the Rabatana, the Norman tower and the cathedral, successively exerted their domination over a dispossessed peasantry. He had started to write an autobiographical novel, *L'uva puttanella*, but died before its completion.

The 'strumpet grape' of the title is a metaphor of the *mezzogiorno*: small, tart yet ripe, so it has to be pressed to contribute to the wine. It was ever thus. 'No one has come to this land,' wrote Levi, 'except as an enemy, a conqueror, or a visitor devoid of understanding'. Even after Lucania declared itself part of the kingdom of Italy, following an uprising in Potenza in 1860, things hardly improved for the *contadini*. Vast areas of land which had formerly belonged to the church were confiscated and sold off to a small number of rich aristocratic families, and so the region's poverty increased and its population dwindled. The peasants who leased land largely from absentee landlords were ruthlessly pursued by their agents for the debts which they inevitably incurred; the land they farmed was poor, the taxes they paid iniquitous, starvation a tragically common experience, malaria endemic.

These were the conditions against which Rocco Scotellaro rebelled. The sudden, unexpected death of his father in 1942, the bombing of Rome, the increased demands now made on him by his family, his commitment to the anti-fascist Union of Resistance, meant that he would not complete his law studies. After the war he joined the Socialist party and became a union organiser, heavily involved in militant action for land reform. Confrontations between farm workers and the police were frequent and often bloody. In 1949, in Montescaglioso, villagers occupied hitherto unworked land on the Lacava estates; the police suddenly occupied the place at two in the morning, cut off the electricity and began a house-to-house search. The workers gathered in the main street and tried to march out of the village. A policeman was knocked over and retaliated by opening fire on the crowd. Giuseppe Novello was killed. Scotellaro's moving poem 'Montescaglioso' honours his sacrifice. For him, poetry was often allied to direct political action, giving a voice to the rootless in search of work, exposing the awful realities of the neglected south.

At the age of 23 Scotellaro became Tricarico's first Socialist mayor. Among his important achievements was the foundation of the town's first hospital. It was set up in a wing of the bishop's palace, thanks to the mediation of the bishop's personal physician, Professor Rocco Mazzarone, a doctor and university professor. It remains a matter of dispute and conjecture in the town even today how an agreement could be reached between a radical socialist and an eminent Catholic prelate. The portrait of Scotellaro which appears on the cover of this collection was painted by Carlo Levi as a preliminary work for his famous large canvas *Lucania '61*, and still hangs in the home of the late Professor, to whose two sisters we are enormously grateful for their permission to reproduce it here.

His political opponents had thought that, given his young age, his low social status and the precarious financial position of this now fatherless family, Scotellaro could be easily manipulated. This proved not to be the case. He was arrested on trumped-up charges of bribery and fraud and imprisoned in Matera. Thanks to the unstinting efforts of Carlo Levi and to the impartial presiding magistrate he was released after 45 days, without charge, a recognition that he had been the victim of a political vendetta. He had, however, become profoundly disillusioned, and his defeat at the provincial elections led him to resign the mayoralty. He was offered a position in the research centre set up by a veteran of the anti-fascist opposition, Professor Manlio Rossi Doria, in the Agricultural Faculty of the university at Portici, working there for the last three years of his life on a project researching illiteracy in Lucania. During this time he also began the first draft of *Contadini del Sud*, a series of biographical case studies of the lives of southern farmworkers commissioned by the publishing house, Laterza, and published in the year after his death. His poetic output continued to be prolific and he explored new avenues, writing *stornelli* or short popular lyrics, poems in dialect, epigrams, and translations. The latter are a particularly poignant indication of Scotellaro's state of mind at this time: there is an elegiac thread running through the poems he chose about the loss of love, absence and separation, the approach of death, poems by Catullus, Goethe, Robert Louis Stevenson, Edgar Lee Masters and Edward Arlington Robinson.

After his death Scotellaro became a legend in the area. Many peasants refused to believe he had died at all. In their homes his portrait hung by the side of images of the saints. On the anniversary of his death the following words were inscribed on the wall of his own house: *il poeta della libertà contadina*, and he is remembered in Tricarico with enormous affection and veneration to this day. Levi recognised some of the qualities in his friend and described them in an essay he wrote about Scotellaro's novel *L'Uva Puttanella*: how the peasants considered Rocco (as the people of Tricarico still call him) to be truly their representative and their brother, not only as a poet and because he stood by them during their land occupations, but because he shared their emotional world, their doubts, the anguish of solitude, their sense of abandonment; his vulnerability exists in his poems side by side with his radicalism.

This year sees the 90th anniversary of his birth, the 60th of his death, and his call still keeps us awake. Many of the same inequalities and divisions between the north and the south of Italy persist, and they are also played out on the global stage between the rich, industrialised countries and the poor, developing ones. Aware of the dangers of stasis and apathy, Scotellaro celebrates the warmth and regenerative power of friendship and loyalty as antidotes to the alienation which technological progress can bring and the inhumanity which blinkered and untrammelled power can impose. In 'È fatto giorno' ('It's light now'), written in the year before he died, he expresses his vision for the enlightenment which he believed would deliver that 'lost legend' and 'a night no longer dark and silent'.

Caroline Maldonado and Allen Prowle

Il giardino dei poveri

È cresciuto il basilico
nel giardino dei poveri:
hanno rubata l'aria alle finestre
su due tavole hanno seminato.

Verranno i passeri,
verranno le mosche,
nel giardino dei poveri.

Ora quando non sai che fare
prendi la brocca in mano,
io ti vedrò cresciuta tra le rose
del giardino dei poveri.

Potenza, 21 ottobre 1948

The Garden of the Poor

The basil has grown
in the garden of the poor:
they have robbed the windows of air,
sowed the seeds on two boards.

The sparrows will come,
the flies will come,
in the garden of the poor.

Now when you don't know what to do
pick up the pitcher in your hand,
then I will see you grown among the roses
in the garden of the poor.

Potenza, 21 October 1948

Alla figlia del trainante

Io no so più viverti accanto
qualcuno mi lega la voce nel petto
sei la figlia del trainante
che mi toglie il respiro sulla bocca.
Perché qui sotto di noi nella stalla
i muli si muovono nel sonno,
perché tuo padre sbuffa a noi vicino
e non ancora va alto sul carro
a scacciare le stelle con la frusta.

1947

To the Carter's Daughter

I cannot live beside you any longer,
something stifles my voice.
You are the carter's daughter
and you take away my breath.
Because below us in the stable
the mules are restless, though asleep,
because your father snoring near us
has not yet clambered on his cart
to beat away the stars with his whip.

1947

Le girandole occhieggiavano a noi

Le girandole occhieggiavano a noi
dal ciglione ove le stuzzicava
il fuochista arrossato dalla miccia.
Oggi sei partita, mia compagna
forestiera, con la festa finita.
La notte di ieri i clarini
al tempo degli scoppi e le voci
delle famiglie sedute alla piazza
e le nostre fitte e calde
sul margine buio della villa.
Ridirle l'altra festa di Settembre,
il gualanello troverà padrone,
avrà la giubba nuova nella fiera!
Quanti giocolieri e merciai
non sono venuti a frugare le tasche
dei cafoni abbelliti!
Tu pure ti porti arreso il mio cuore.
Per me il tuo volto bianco di città
ripete il gioco di queste luci:
hanno disfatto di fretta gl'impianti,
i camion scapanno come alla deriva,
i ragazzi s'affannano a cercare
è da stamane la bomba viva.

settembre 1947

The Catherine Wheels

The Catherine wheels stared at us
from the bank where the firework man
poked at them, his face ruddy from the fuse.
Today you've gone back, my foreign friend,
now the festival is over.
Last night, the clarinets
together with the bangs and the voices
of the families sitting round the square,
and our own, thick and warm,
on the dark edge of the villa.
If I could only tell her again of the other September festival,
when the farmhand will find a new master
and get a new jacket at the fair!
How many of the jugglers and haberdashers
have come to fleece the pockets
of the spruced-up peasants!
You too steal away the heart I gave up to you.
For me your white city face
repeats the play of these lights:
they've taken down the stalls in a hurry,
trucks drift away,
the boys are busy hunting around,
since this morning for the live bomb.

September 1947

Una fucsia

Una fucsia in mano avevi
come tengono i gigli
le immagini di Sant'Antonio.
Per un simile fiore che mi desti
si svegliarono in me le feste
massacranti del paese
quando le bande vengono chiamate
da un colpo sul luogo dei fuochi
accesi nel cielo e vince la gara
l'incendio più fresco di fucsia.
Anche mi ricordo un anno fa
i pennacchi della pula sulle aie.
Ecco, il paese ti porto in città.

1948

A Fuchsia

You held a fuchsia in your hand
like Saint Anthony's images
hold lilies.
Because you gave me a flower like this,
it roused in me a memory
of those madcap village festivals
when the bands are summoned by a bang
to the place where fireworks light the sky
and the prize is won
by the brightest fuchsia blaze.
I remember too, a year ago,
the plumes of chaff on the threshing floor.
See, I bring you the country in the city.

1948

Ce ne dovevamo andare

Tu non te ne volevi più andare,
contammo le luci del'anfiteatro
deboli occhi attorno a noi.
Per i densi profumi della menta
levandoci dicesti:
-Lascia che guardi ancora questo posto.
E come lo dicesti
i capelli ti scesero sul viso.
Ce ne dovevamo andare
perché nascemmo altrove
sotto le mura di cinta lontane
di due sante cittadelle.
Il suo carcere spettava ad ognuno,
ad ognuno il suo vagone
ci portarono in traduzione.
A Rimini campo neutro
crescemmo il nostro amore
dove i putti del tempio
ignari si toccana i nudi
sul mare turchino.
Nelle tue piane del Nord
dove ti sei fermata?
A chi risolvi la tua gioia di amare?
Io mi sono lasciato andare
nei sentieri affondati dai carri.
Ora noi ci parliamo tra le sbarre.

1948

We Should Have Left

You no longer wanted to leave.
We counted the amphitheatre's lights,
pale eyes surrounding us.
Through the dense scents of mint
you said as we got up
-let me look at this place a little longer-
And as you said it
your hair fell over your face.
We should have left
because we were born elsewhere,
under the far off encircling walls
of two holy citadels.
We each had a prison
and each a prison van,
they took us back.
At Rimini, a neutral ground,
we let our love grow
where the *putti* of the Tempio
on the deep blue sea
touched, naked, unknowing.
On your Northern plains
where did you stop?
With whom do you satisfy your joy of loving?
I let myself go
along the paths worn down by carts.
Now we talk to each other through bars.

1948

Le foglie delle palme d'ulivo

Sovrastano sguaiate cornacchie
sui fumi dei comignoli in marzo.
Accendiamo per le nostre zitelle
le foglie delle palme d'ulivo:
morse sobbalzano, anime penanti,
dicono di sì e di no
alle nostre turbate domande.

Le Palme del 1948

The Leaves of the Olive Palms

Vulgar crows circle above
the smoking chimneys in March.
For our unmarried women we burn
the leaves of the olive palms:
flame-bitten they writhe, tortured souls;
to our questions
they say yes, they say no.

Palm Sunday 1948

A una madre

Come vuoi bene a una madre
che ti cresce nel pianto
sotto la ruota violenta della Singer
intenta ai corredi nuziali
e a rifinire le tomaie alte
delle donne contadine?

Mi sganciarono dalla tua gonna
pollastrello comprato alla sua chioccia.
Mi mandasti fuori nella strada
con la mia faccia.
La mia faccia lentigginosa ha il segno
delle tue voglie di gravida
e me la tengo in pegno.

Tu ora vorresti da me
amore che non ti so dare.
Siamo due inquilini nella casa
che ci teniamo in dispetto,
ti vedo sempre tesa
a rubarmi un po' di affetto.
Tu che a moine no mi hai avvezzato.

Una per sempre io ti ho benvoluta
quando venne l'altro figlio di papà:
nacque da un amore in fuga,
fu venduto a due sposi sterili
che facevano i contadini
in un paese vicino.
Allora alzasti per noi lo stesso letto
e ci chiamavi Rocco tutt'e due.

1948

To a Mother

How do you love a mother
who brings you up in tears
under the furious wheel of the Singer,
always so busy with trousseaux
and with finishing off the uppers
of peasant women's shoes?

They unhooked me from your skirt,
young cockerel bought from its mother hen.
You sent me out into the street
with nothing to show except my face,
whose freckles are the marks
of what you craved when pregnant.
I hold it as a pledge.

I cannot give you now
the love you want from me.
We two are the tenants of the house,
we live together with no joy.
I see you always intent on
robbing me of a little affection.
You who never taught me sweet words.

I first, and forever after, cared for you
when papa's other son arrived.
Born of a love affair in flight,
he was sold to a childless couple
who were working on the land
in a village near our own.
You then set up one bed for the two of us
and gave the name Rocco to us both.

1948

Mio padre

Mio padre misurava il piede destro
vendeva le scarpe fatte da maestro
nelle fiere piene di polvere.

    Tagliava con la roncella
    la suola come il pane
    una volta fece fuori le budella
    a un figlio di cane.
    Fu in una notte da non ricordare
    e quando gli si chiedeva di parlare
    faceva gli occhi piccoli a tutti.

A mio fratello tirava i pesi addosso
che non sapeva scrivere
i reclami delle tasse.
Aveva nelle maniche pronto
sempre un trincetto tagliente
era per la pancia dell'Agente.
Mise lui la pulce nell'orecchio
al suo compagno che fu arrestato
perché un giorno disperato
mandò all'ufficio il suo banchetto
e sopra c'era un biglietto:
'Occhi di buoi
fatigate voi'.

    Allora non sperò più
    mio padre ciabattino
    con riso fragile e senza rossore
    rispondeva da un gradino
    'Sia sempre lodato' a un monsignore.
    E si mise già stanco -
    dal largo mantello gli uscivano gli occhi -
    a posare sulla piazza, di fianco,
    a difesa degli uomini che stavano a crocchi.

My Father

My father would measure the right foot
and sell shoes made by a master of the craft
at fairs amid clouds of dust.

> With his cobbler's knife he cut
> the sole like a loaf of bread
> and once spilled the guts
> of a son of a bitch.
> It was not a night to recall
> and when they wanted him to talk about it
> he would just scowl at them all.

He threw the scales at my brother
who never could write down
the tax returns.
He always kept up his sleeve
a blade ready sharpened
for the tax man's paunch.
It was he who planted doubt in the mind of his friend
who got himself arrested
when one day in despair
he sent his bench to the tax office
together with a note:
'Now you, owl eyes,
can wear yourself out.'

> By then he had lost all hope,
> my shoemaker father.
> From one of the steps he replied
> to a monsignor, 'May He always be praised,'
> with a quiet laugh and without a blush.
> And already tired, his eyes
> peering over his ample cloak,
> he defended the men gathered in groups
> and stood on the square by their side.

E morì – come volle – di subito,
senza fare la pace col mondo.
Quando avvertì l'attacco
cercò la mano di mamma nel letto,
gliela stritolava, e lei capì e si ritrasse.
Era steso con la faccia stravolta,
gli era rimasta nella gola
la parola della rivolta.

Poi dissero ch'era un brav'uomo,
anche l'agente, e gli fecero frastuono.

1948

And he died – as he had wished to – suddenly,
his peace still not made with the world.
When he felt the attack
he reached for mamma's hand in the bed,
he squeezed it, and she understood and pulled back.
They stretched him out, his face distorted,
words of revolt still in his throat.

>Then they said what a fine man he was,
>even the tax-man, and they made such a fuss.

1948

Natale

Si cammina su e giù
lungo le stazioni e queste vie.
C'è chi mi dice: Abbandona la nebbia,
abbandona l'asfalto grasso,
le vetrine: luce di dieci candele
pende su baschi e giocattoli.
Le mie famiglie riempiono le case,
hanno lasciato la tavola intatta
per il bambino della mezzanotte.

1949

Christmas

They walk up and down
past stations and along these streets.
There is one who says to me: leave behind the fog,
the slippery asphalt,
the shop windows: light from ten candles
slants down on berets and on toys.
My families fill the houses;
they have left untouched the table set
for the child of midnight.

1949

Tu non ci fai dormire cuculo disperato

Tutt'intorno le montagne brune
è ricresciuto il tuo colore
Settembre amico delle mie contrade.
Ti sei cacciato in mezzo a noi,
t'hanno sentito accanto le nostre donne
quando naufraghi grilli
dalle ristoppie arse del paese
si sollevano alle porte con un grido.
E c'è verghe di fichi seccati
e i pomidoro verdi sulle volte
e il sacco del grano duro, il mucchio
delle mandorle abbattute.

Tu no ci fai dormire
cuculo disperato,
col tuo richiamo:
Sì, ridaremo i passi alle trazzere,
ci metteremo alle fatiche domani
che i fiumi ritorneranno gialli
sotto i calanchi
e il vento ci turbinerà
i mantelli negli armadi.

1 settembre 1947

Despairing Cuckoo, Your Call Keeps Us Awake

All round the brown mountains
your colour has come back,
our old September friend.
You've settled in among us.
Our women have heard you quite close
when castaway crickets
fleeing the burnt stubble of our fields
rise up and screech at the doors.
From the ceilings hang
strings of dried figs and green tomatoes;
there's a sack of hard wheat,
a heap of felled almonds.

Despairing cuckoo,
your call
keeps us awake:
yes, we'll trudge back along the paths
and tomorrow get down to work
when water streams yellow again
under the furrows,
and the wind billows
our coats in the cupboards.

1 September 1947

Ti rubarono a noi come una spiga

per un giovane amico assassinato

Vide la morte con gli occhi e disse:
Non mi lasciate morire
con la testa sull'argine
della rotabile bianca.
Non passano che corriere
veloci e traini lenti
ed autocarri pieni di carbone.
Non mi lasciate con la testa
sull'argine recisa da una falce.
Non lasciatemi la note
con una coperta sugli occhi
tra due carabinieri
che montano di guardia.
Non so chi m'ha ucciso
portatemi a casa,
i contadini come me
si ritirano in fila nelle squadre
portatemi sul letto
dov'è morta mia madre.
O mettetevi qui attorno a ballare
e succhiate una goccia del mio sangue
di me vi farà dimenticare.
Lungo è aspettare l'aurora e la legge
domani anche il gregge
fuggirà questo pascolo bagnato.
E la mia testa la vedrete, un sasso
rotolare nelle notti
per la cinta delle macchie.
Così la morte ci fa nemici!
Così una falce taglia netto!
(Che male vi ho fatto?)
Ci faremo scambievole paura.

They Stole You from Us Like an Ear of Corn

for a young friend murdered

He saw death with his eyes and said:
do not leave me here to die
with my head on the verge
of the white roadway.
Nothing passes by, except fast
buses and slow wagons
and lorries filled with coal.
Do not leave me on the roadside,
with my head severed by a sickle.
Do not leave me here at night
with a blanket covering my eyes,
between two policemen
mounting guard.
I do not know who killed me.
Carry me back home.
Peasants like me
withdraw in line into their ranks.
Carry me to the bed
in which my mother died.
Oh, gather round me here to dance
and suck a drop of my blood,
it will drive me from your mind.
It is too long to wait for dawn, and for the law.
Tomorrow the flock too
will flee this sodden pasture.
And at night you will see my head,
a stone rolling
around the plot of stains.
In this way death makes us enemies!
In this way a sickle cuts clean through!
(What harm did I do you?)
We will strike fear into each other's hearts.

Nel tempo che il grano matura
al ronzare di questi rami
avremmo cantata, amici, insieme.
E il vecchio mio padre
non si taglierà le vene
a mietere da solo
i campi di avena?

1948

At the time when the grain ripens,
at the humming of these branches,
we would have sung together as friends.
And my old father,
will he not cut through his veins
now that he has to harvest alone
the fields of oats?

1948

I santi contadini di Matera

Anima di lupo antico
assassinato davanti le porte
il giorno della fame più crudele,
vicina ti ridesti a noi soffusa
nel tuono del tristo orologio
e brami pane e cipolla, e miele
all'ultima ferita del corvo.
E che strazio nell'aria le campane
che ci pungono d'aghi il nostro cuore!
Che vogliono da noi?
Fanno paura agl'innocenti
come ai fanciulli beati
gli ultimi fiati del macello.
Finitela, benedette campane!
Con questi venti nei nostri tuguri
svegliate la faccia dei morti violenti
e ci fate più lupi di prima.
E voi date una mano
perché l'avranno interrata profonda
la pupa della fattucchiera
nella Gravina che circonda
i santi contadini di Matera!

Matera, 3 marzo 1948

The Peasant Saints of Matera

Spirit of the ancient wolf
murdered before the doors
on the day of cruellest hunger,
neighbour, you laughed at us
as you melted into the booming of the mournful clock
and craved bread and onion, and honey
for the ultimate wound of the crow.
And what an agony in the air the church bells
which prick our hearts with needles!
What is it they want from us?
They strike fear in the innocent
as do the dying breaths of that slaughter
in children who are blessed.
Be done with it, holy bells!
With these winds blowing through our hovels
bring back life to those who died a violent death
and make us more wolf than before.
And lend us a hand
for they will have buried
the witch's doll deep down
in the Gravina that winds round
the peasant saints of Matera!

Matera, 3 March 1948

E ci mettiamo a maledire insieme

La stagione che alimenta
l'orgasmo tutto nostro è questa:
dai rosmarini bianchi di polvere
dai fischi delle rondini ai nidi.
Siamo nel mese innanzi alla raccolta:
brutto umore all'uomo sulla piazza
appena al variare dei venti
e le donne si muovono dalle case
capitane di vendetta.
Gridano al Comune di volere
il tozzo di pane e una giornata
e scarpe e strade e tutto.
E ci mettiamo a maledire insieme,
il sindaco e le rondini e le donne,
e il nostro urlo si fa più forte
come quello della massaia che ha sperso
la gallina e bandisce alle strade
solitarie il suo rancore,
come quello di borea che si sente
soffiando basso alla fiamma del sole
ora cresce le molli spighe alla falce.

1947

And Together We Let Out Our Curses

This is the time of year which drives us
to a frenzy all our own:
of rosemary white with dust,
of the whistling of swallows in the nest.
We are in the month before harvest:
the slightest shift of winds
and the men on the square turn nasty,
women leave their houses,
vendetta's leaders.
At the town hall they scream their want,
a crust of bread, a day's work,
and shoes and roads and everything.
And together, mayor and swallows and women,
we let out our curses
which grow louder,
like that of the housewife who has lost
her hen and who tells everyone of her anger
in the empty streets,
like that of the north wind
blowing low at the sun's flame,
raising the limp corn-stalks to our scythes.

1947

Era la cavalcata della Bruna

Festa della Madonna della Bruna a Matera

Afflitti ulivi
sui tuffi di Matera.
O gli amari poemi
delle morte stagioni!

È una notte che fugge la faina
coi suoi occhi di brace.
E gli antenati ecco sentirsi in canti
per la campagna acquattata:
erano i cafoni in quadrigliè,
passava la cavalcata della Bruna
a risvegliare le caverne
sui bordi della roccie
al di là della collina,
era il silenzio dell'acqua infossata
che faceva tuonare la Gravina.

1947

It Was the Cavalcade of the Bruna

Festival of the Madonna della Bruna at Matera

Tormented olive trees
on Matera's *tufa* crags.
Oh the bitter poems
of dead seasons!

It is a night when the stone marten flees,
its eyes like embers,
and our ancestors hear themselves again
in songs all over the stunted country:
they were the peasants who wore checked cloth.
The cavalcade of the Bruna passed this way
to awaken the caves
on the edges of the rocks
beyond the hill.
It was the silence of sunken water
that made the gorge of the Gravina thunder.

1947

Olimpiadi

I nostri padri furono fanciulli
lesti e furiosi e giganti nei giuochi.
Dettero mano alle roccie, lassù nell'aria
la terra com'era fredda e lontana.

Li misero caterve sulle chiatte,
loro, di sdegno, spaccarono l'oceano.

Affilaste le pietre nelle terre,
padri, desti al rantolo degli animali,
provando i denti alla scorza degli alberi.

I nostri padri furono fanciulli
che vennero a stare ai lidi, sui monti
e si misero a cantare.
In faccia al mar Jonio, nei giorni più lunghi
a Olimpia chiamavano il loro Dio,
erano dei la terra il cielo il mare,
e Omero li sentì, quel povero
che a Cuma chiese un truogolo di crusca.

O Gesù,
ti piacque il giuoco del pane e del vino,
che piace anche a noi.
A Cuma il vecchio cieco
a Napoli, a New York un giovane cantore
bussa alle porte con i denti in bocca.

Girotondo fanciulli e padri,
i mirabili giuochi nei tempi
sulle nostre zolle! Cantammo alle torri,
alle sorgive, nei punti estremi
le nostre voci serene.

Olympics

Our fathers were children,
fast and furious and giants in their games.
They put their hands to rocks, and high up in the wind
the land was so cold, so far away.

Down there they loaded up their barges
that scornfully cleaved the ocean.

You sharpened stones from the ground, fathers,
aware of the animals' dying groans,
testing your teeth on the bark of trees.

Our fathers were children
who came to settle on the shores, on the mountains,
and began to sing.
Facing the Ionian, on the longest days,
they called out to their God at Olympia.
Their gods were the land, the sky, the sea,
and Homer heard them, that pauper
who begged for a trough of bran at Cumae.

Oh, Jesus,
you enjoyed the game of bread and wine
and we enjoy it too.
In Cumae the blind old man;
in Naples, in New York, showing his teeth
a young singer knocks on doors.

Ring-a-ring-a-roses children and their fathers,
marvellous games in their times
on our clods of earth! We sang to the towers,
to the springs, our clear voices
reached the remotest places.

O miei padri morti e tranquilli,
ancora il mondo crolla
nell'occhio dei fanciulli.
Resta a cantare chi è sempre povero,
e grida a un'ora di notte il nonno,
lui, l'atleta delle feste al tramonto
cadde dall'albero della cuccagna.

1949

O my fathers, dead and in peace,
the world crumbles again
before the eyes of children.
The eternally poor stay behind to sing
and at some time in the night grandad shouts out,
he, the athlete at feasts, slipped down
from the tree of Cockayne as the sun was setting.

1949

Monelli

Le fila di gru
che accendono d'urli il nostro cielo
non le vidi più.
Tutte le rondini nere ci lasciano
nell'orizzonte corto del quartiere.
Noi mozziamo le ali
alle colombe selvaggie:
con cauto amore incappano sui tetti.

1942-43

Brats

You see no more
the flights of cranes
that sear our sky with screams.
All the black swallows are leaving us
on the narrow skyline of our district.
We clip the wings
of the wild doves:
with wary love they bump together on rooftops.

1942-43

Camminano sulle zampe dei gatti

Improvvisa la sera chi ha toccati
me, le mie carte, la pezza di luce
sui mattoni della stanza.
È tanto imbrunito
che mi sento addosso paura.
Ha ripreso la vita
dei piccoli rumori.
Sono sui tetti le anime
dei morti del vicinato,
camminano sulle zampe dei gatti.

Tricarico, iuglio 1945

They Walk on Cats' Paws

Suddenly evening has touched us:
me, my papers, the patch of light
on the tiled floor of my room.
It has become so dark
that I am filled with fear.
The life of smallest sounds
has now returned.
Over the rooftops, the souls
of the neighbourhood's dead
walk on cats' paws.

Tricarico, July 1945

Verde giovinezza

C'è tempo quando abbondano
lucertole nelle vigne
e a qualcuna nuova coda inazzurra,
quando nei campi spuntano covoni
impazienti di fuoco
e la cicala assorda e mi tappa
l'orecchio alle campane, alle canzoni,
al lungo richiamo di mamma
che mi rivuole vicino e suo.
Quando la fiumara è bianca....
Allora mi voglio scolare l'orciuolo
e coricarmi in terra
senza memoria più
della verde giovinezza.

1945

Green Youth

There is a time when the vines
are alive with lizards,
some with new tails tinted blue,
when impatient corn sheaves in the fields
sprout up like flames
and the cicada deafens and stops me hearing
the bells, the songs,
the drawn out calling of my mother
who wants me back, wants me hers.
When the torrent is white…
then I want to drain the jug
and lie down on the ground
with no more memories
of green youth.

1945

I Lucani cantano monotoni

Urla la nostra canzone araba
perché solo agli zingari
noi abbiamo creduto.
Gli zingari rubano
le mandrie ai padroni
e noi cantiamo cantiamo
nella notte con loro.
Il re degli zingari è con noi
mangia con noi la carne rubata.
E noi cantiamo le lodi
solo al re degli zingari.
La donna zingara è la più bella
di quante donne che ci hanno guardato.
E noi cantiamo le grazie
delle femmine belle.
Gli animali degli zingari
hanno l'occhio mansueto
dei compagni di viaggio.
E noi compriamo i cavalli
che ci vendono gli zingari.
E solo gli zingari
ci fanno ridere e piangere
così per diletto.
Il fuoco degli zingari nel petto
le notti che il nostro tamburo
aduna i cafoni lucani
battendo nel viottolo scuro.

1948

The Monotonous Singing of the Lucanians

Our Arabic song howls
because we only ever trusted
the gypsies.
The gypsies steal
herds from their masters.
And we sing we sing
through the night with them.
The king of the gypsies is with us.
With us he eats stolen meat.
And we only sing the praises
of the king of the gypsies.
The lady gypsy is the most beautiful
of all the women who have looked at us.
And we sing the graces
of beautiful women.
The gypsies' animals
have the docile eyes
of travelling companions.
And we buy the horses
that the gypsies sell us.
And only gypsies
make us laugh and cry
just out of joy.
Gypsy fire in the breast
on nights that our drum
summons the Lucanian peasants,
beating along the dark alley.

1948

Biglietto per Torino

Torino larga di cuore
sei una fanciulla, mi prendi la mano.
Io mi ero messo in cammino:
mi hanno mandato lontano,
qui, gente che ti sogna come me
nel vento delle Fiat.
Mi hanno coccolato sulle ginocchia
i duri miei padri saraceni,
ridacchiavano alle mie stornellate;
mi facevano saltare come un pupo
le belle donne nere.

Un giorno li vidi piangere,
c'erano dei tuoni scuri nell'aria
e non sapevano piangere
con quelle faccie dure.
E io sulle ginocchia cantai un'altra canzone.
Allora mi tennero a terra, dissero:
-Va là, sai camminare da solo.
Con quanta lena me ne son venuto
a toccare l'azzurro delle tute:
voglio dirlo a quegli altri, ai saraceni.

1949

Ticket for Turin

Turin, big of heart,
you're a young girl, you take my hand.
I set off on my journey:
they sent me away,
here, where people dream of you
as I do, in the Fiats' stream of wind.
They fondled me on their knees,
my hard Saracen fathers,
would laugh at the rhymes that I made up;
just like a puppet they would make me jump,
the dark beautiful women.

One day I saw them weep,
dark thunder rumbled in the air,
and they did not know how to weep
with those hard faces of theirs,
and on their knees I sang another song.
So they put me on the ground and said:
go on, you can walk now on your own.
How keen I was when I came to touch
the working men's blue overalls:
I want to tell them that, those Saracens.

1949

La ginestra

Vergine col canestro che ridai
la ginestra ai santi,
non si sentono pianti più muti dei tuoi:
che farà quella mano tesa d'argento
che sollevano a benedire la campagna?
Le fatiche, e le spighe e le viti in gola al vento,
s'aprirà ai morti la castagna?
O bella col canestro che canti e porti
ginestre ai vivi, ginestre ai morti.

1951

Broom

Virgin with the basket
carrying broom back to the saints,
no weeping is more silent than yours:
what will your stiff silver hand do
when it is raised to bless the countryside?
The exhaustion, and ears of corn and vines in the wind's throat,
will the chestnut split open to the dead?
O beautiful lady with the basket, singing,
bringing broom for the living, broom for the dead.

1951

Viaggio di ritorno

La mamma cammina
dai letti al focolare,
passeggia sotto e sopra
l'aratore in collina.

Mamma, alzerò le mura della casa,
il gallo del camino canterà sulle tegole,
e tu te ne sarai già andata.

Acqua passata
il logoro giornale d'Italia
a chi dice più niente.
Me ne ritorno alla mia terra nuda.

Tra paese e città la terra nuda,
il silenzio della campana
e una voce quanto più lontana.

1951

Return Journey

Mother walks
from the beds to the hearth,
the ploughman paces the hill
above and beneath.

I will raise up the house walls, mother,
the weathercock will crow on the roof-tiles
and you will be gone already.

Water under the bridge,
the jaded newspaper of Italy
with nothing more to say to anyone.
I'm returning to my stripped land.

From village to town the stripped land,
the church bell silent
and a voice how much more distant.

1951

Il grano del sepolcro

È cigliato nello stipo il grano
del sepolcro per Gesù bendato.
Verrà giugno, morirà anche mia madre,
voglio portarle spighe spigolate
dentro il suo scialle sacro
che per altro non avrò toccato.
Allora la casa sarà la via che mi mantiene:
non morire, mamma mia, che ti vorrò più bene.

Portici, marzo 1951

The Grain for the Sepulchre

The grain for the sepulchre of the blindfolded Christ
has sprouted in the cupboard.
June will come, my mother will die.
I want to bring her ears of corn just gleaned
and wrapped up in her sacred shawl
which I would not otherwise have touched.
Then home will be the road I follow:
Mamma, do not die, so I may love you more.

Portici, March 1951

Lo scoglio di Positano

Più paura che della morte
se si rompono gli amici e gli amori.
Fratelli e sorelle della mia corte
siete qui, vi conto, nessuno è fuori.

Li Galli se ne sono andati
e la Punta Licosa
nella notte del mare.
Come ti voglio amare
fin che dura lo scoglio e la paura.

Positano, 28 ottobre 1951 e Portici, 1-2 novembre 1951

The Crags of Positano

Breaking away from friends and loved ones
is more frightening than death.
My band of brothers and sisters,
all of you are here, I count you, no one is left out.

Gone are the Galli
and Licosa Point
into the sea's night.
How I want, dear one, to love you
as long as the crags last, as long as fear.

Positano, 28 October 1951 and Portici, 1-2 November 1951

Notte in campagna

Coricàti ai piedi dell'olmo,
il cielo ha meno stelle per il vento.
Le Pleiadi sono incenerite,
l'Orsa è sgangherata
sull'orizzonte pulito.

Io voglio te, niente boccali di vino forte
né l'origano e il sale sul pane.
Tu distesa rimani
ferita da non so chi ti ha giocato a sorte.

1949

Night in the Country

Bed yourself down at the foot of the elm,
the sky has fewer stars because of the wind.
The Pleiades are all burned out,
the Great Bear is shambling
over the clear line of the horizon.

I want you. Not strong wine in my tankard,
nor oregano or salt on my bread.
Still you lie spread out
hurt by whoever drew lots for you.

1949

Costiera Amalfitana

Mare celeste di pozzi blu e lattee correnti,
l'abito di foglie del carrubo ti segna,
piega all'ansito tuo piano e indifferente
la sua chioma di onde sulle roccie violate e coperte.

L'amore non chiede nulla, né frutti né serti
nel giorno che ha colori aggrovigliati e soli,
nella notte quando cade l'abbondanza del cielo
fino al piede alla marina punta di lampare.

Te sola vorrei amare, bambina che ora spunti
e hai la piccolezza dell'arancia verde
e dovrai ingiallire per avere la mia età.

È sbocciata la silenziosa regina di una notte
che affascina il muro vecchio come una lampada
e l'alba tra un'ora la richiuderà
amante insonne affogata nei sepali biondi.

E noi fiorire e morire e religioso andare,
ognuno nel suo turno di stagione,
nei giorni e nelle notti senz'amore.

1952

Amalfi Coast

Pale blue sea with darker-coloured pools and milky streams
and you streaked by the carob's dress of leaves,
to the even and indifferent rhythm of your breath
the waves' long hair is folded over sunken, violated rocks.

Love asks for nothing, neither fruits nor garlands,
in daytime when colours merge or stand alone,
by night when the sky's abundance tumbles down
to the shoreline pricked with fishermen's lamps.

You only are the love I want, little girl still growing up;
you have the smallness of the still green orange,
and will need to turn yellow to be of my age.

The silent queen of night has bloomed
charming the old wall like lamplight
and in an hour's time the dawn will close her up,
sleepless lover drowning among blond sepals.

Our lot to flower and die, departing blessed,
each one in turn, to each their season,
throughout the days and nights, loveless.

1952

Ripresa

Le chiome degli alberi a marzo
sono mani perlate di giovani.
Non si cresce, lo sapete, in amore:
è sempre per giovani e vecchi uno sfarzo.

Da Solopaca a Poggioreale
fischiano treni e uccelli
alle case sparse, nidi e stazioni,
agli uomini che portano le pale.

Qui vicino cresce un nuovo quartiere,
dodici bambini che non vanno a scuola
tengono ai Granili un cantiere,
chi porta i tufi e chi tiene la cazzuola.

Il vecchio barcaiuolo parla del gabbiano
che non ha il nido né a terra né a mare.
All'orologio pare la tarantola
con le zampe alle sei e venticinque,
la mattina di sole ricomincia.

Portici, 24-25 February 1953

Starting Again

In March the crowns of trees
are like the pearly hands of youths.
You know, you don't grow into love:
for young and old there's always an abundance.

From Solopaca to Poggioreale
trains and birds whistle
at scattered houses, nests and stations,
at men carrying shovels.

Here, close by, a new neighbourhood springs up,
a dozen children who do not go to school
work on a building site at the Granili,
one carries tufa blocks, another the trowel.

The old boatman tells of the seagull
which has no nest either on land or sea.
The tarantula appears on the clock,
its feet at twenty-five past six,
the sun's morning starts again.

Portici, 24-25 February 1953

Ora che ti ho perduta

Ora che ti ho perduta come una pietra preziosa
so che non ti ho mai avuta né spina né rosa:
non stavi al fondo della cassa che sarebbe bastato
alzare panni e coperte per rivederti a posto
con pena e occhi incerti nella massa delle cose.
Ti portavo addosso con carte e matite e monete
e sapevo di perderti ma non come pietra preziosa,
credevo che tant'acqua poteva levarmi la sete.
Ora, che voglio fare?, guardare dove non c'eri
dove non sei dove non sarai coi tuoi occhi neri.

Positano, 17 giugno 1953

Now That I Have Lost You

Now that I have lost you like a precious stone
I know you were never mine, neither rose nor thorn:
you were not at the bottom of the trunk where,
just by lifting blankets, coats, I'd see you in your place again,
your sorrow too, your eyes unsure among the mass of things.
I took you with me, with my paper, pencils, coins,
knowing I would lose you, but not like a precious stone.
I thought I would slake my thirst with so much water.
What now do I want to do? Look where you never were,
where you are not, will never be, with those dark eyes of yours.

Positano, 17 June 1953

I topi

I topi sentono gli occhi
quando mi sollevo a vederli.
Si muovono con gambe lunghe
di uomo nella stanza.
Resistono perché sanno
che anche io alla fine mi addormento
e per loro sarà libero giuco.

La coda è la grande ala
che raschia e con quella
il topo vola dai buchi
pallottola dall'animo
dei fucili al bersaglio.
O mio cuore antico, topo
solenne che non esci fuori
e non hai libero sfogo
come non l'ha la frana
della città degli uomini accesa e ruotante;
e non senti gli occhi
di chi tra le donne- meno crudele
e meno esitante – pure ti guarda lontana.

13 December 1953

The Rats

The rats feel my eyes
raised to watch them.
They stalk the room,
their long legs like a man's.
They won't give up, they know that in the end
I will fall asleep too,
leaving them free to play.

The tail is the great wing scraping the ground.
With it the rat flies from its hole,
bullet of the soul,
from gun to target.
O ancient heart, solemn rat,
you won't get out.
You can't break loose
any more than can man's fallen
city, wheeling in flame.
Nor do you feel the eyes
of one among women – less cruel,
less unsure – still watching you from afar.

13 December 1953

Pioggia settembrina

ai piccoli di casa

Cielo bigio, l'aria è tetra
dorme il cane alla sua cuccia
tace il vento senza pioggia
ed un bimbo guarda ai vetri
l'uccellino che no c'è.

Forse il vecchio conta i giorni
già da tanto sta nel letto
volerà come la rondine
fuggita dal suo tetto.
Ecco guarda, aspetta, aspetta:
viene pioggia da quei monti.

Ecco cade dal suo ramo
un frutto già maturo,
anche una foglia cade.
Aspetta, aspetta.
Cosa sarà di te?
Cosa sarà di noi?

Quel carretto fermo…
Il fumo del camino…
Un asino che raglia,
i contadini: guancie sulla zappa,
tetra la terra, il cielo bigio.

Tricarico, 1941

September Rain

to the little ones of the house

Sky grey, air leaden,
the dog asleep in his basket,
the wind silent without rain
and a child looks through the window pane
for the little bird that isn't there.

Maybe the old man is counting the days,
he has already been in bed so long,
he will fly like the swallow
that has fled from his roof.
There, look, wait, wait:
rain is coming over these mountains.

There falling from its branch
a fruit, already ripe,
a leaf falls too.
Wait, wait.
What will become of you?
What will become of us?

That pushcart at a standstill…
The chimney smoke…
A braying donkey,
the peasants: cheeks to the hoe,
leaden land, grey sky.

Tricarico, 1941

Canzone tragica

Impallidiva quel volto della luna reverso.
Forse pensava la luna qualcuno
le chiudesse gli occhi e lei non fosse più
per la terra splendente nel cielo turchino.

Viaggiava con ali serrate
un uccello librato nell'aria.
Diradava all'istante
il fumo d'un alto camino.

Il tempo in un ritmo solenne
marcava i secondi
gli stessi secondi
di ogni mattino.

Risalivo nei tempi....
memorie sperdute
leggende fiorivano in mente
di vita vissuta

tra svolazzi d'angeli a schiera
al di là della svolta dei cieli.
Mi guardo attorno e il sole è sorto
e la scena del mondo tramuta.

È quella casa che crollò
di due vecchi giovani sposi
con un figlio ciascuno:
due muri, un'imposta sbattuta.

Tivoli, giugno 1942

Tragic Song

The far side of the moon turned pale.
Perhaps she feared, if someone's eyes were closed,
that she would cease to be
for the radiant earth in the deep-blue sky.

A bird set free into the air
glided on folded wings.
Suddenly the smoke dispersed
from a high chimney.

Time ticked away the seconds
in a solemn rhythm,
the very same seconds
of the start of every day.

Then I went back in time…
lost memories,
legends of a lived life,
grew in my mind

among the fluttering wings of an angel host
beyond the bending of the skies.
I look around me and the sun has come out
and the view of the world has changed.

That is the house that fell down,
the house of two old people, married young,
each with a son:
two walls, a battered shutter.

Tivoli, June 1942

Villa d'Este

Entra che ti sfiora un fresco di vesti di edere
e un ventagliare di fronde.
Che incantano i viali
e svettano i fiori,
scivola l'uccello pei rami;
ondeggiano calme
le vette dei pini
e glicini scendono scendono
con lo scroscio de l'acque.
Da ovunque sui podi
dormono statue,
china la pietra del capo
su ruscelletti cascanti.
Vela il muschio sottile
le pietre abbronzate,
si scende, si scende!
Come quando tra i boschi alla marina
spira solenne riecheggiando il vento.

giugno 1942

Villa d'Este

Enter to feel the cool brush of the ivy's dress
and a fanning of branches.
So the avenues enchant,
flowers come into bloom,
and a bird slips through the boughs;
the tops of pine trees
sway calmly
and down down with the roar of the water
wisteria cascades.
Everywhere statues sleep
on their plinths,
their stone heads lean
over tumbling streams.
Fine moss veils
bronzed stones,
down, down you go!
As when, solemnly, the echoing wind
blows through the woods to the sea.

June 1942

Donne

Per la mia strada già tante
donne vidi passare
belle come nei sogni
lontane stelle che l'occhio
si paga di mirare.
Quella la via delle mie donne
quando s'oscura il giorno
e vaghe forme intorno
dilettano i miei sensi
or che ogni porta s'è rinchiusa
frusciando di gonne.

24 Novembre 1942

Women

Along my road I have seen
so many women pass by
as beautiful as in dreams,
distant stars,
rewards for the eye.
Along my road of women
when day darkens
and vague shapes around me
delight my senses,
the hour when every door is shut,
the rustle of skirts.

24 November 1942

Tempo nostalgico

Una legge impose
alla mia vita un carme:
cercare i miei lidi da me
canti d'arrivi e di partenze.
Ho l'anima sfilacciata a brandelli
per tutti i luoghi più solitari.
Vado rincorrendo fanciulle lontane
per le strade di tutti i paesi.
Mi fingo i vari colori delle valli
e qualche più grave scampanio,
un'aria più assorta,
il declino delle strade affollate
e le canzoni della notte.
È la sosta di casa mia
che compone i brandelli dell'anima.
Quei boschi e le terre di stoppie
s'hanno il mio saluto di pianto
per l'ultimo addio.
Ecco che corre la terra
gli alberi mi dicono addio sciogliendo le chiome
e mi rifaccio altrove a pensare
a quei boschi e le terre di stoppie.

1942

A Time of Nostalgia

A law imposed
an ode on my life:
to search my shores alone,
songs of arrival and departure.
Shreds of my soul now lie
in all the loneliest places.
I chase after distant girls
along the streets of every village.
I adopt the various colours of the valleys,
a more solemn peal of bells,
a more reflective air,
the decay of crowded streets
and songs of the night.
To rest in my own home
binds the shreds of my soul.
Those woods and stubbled fields
receive my tearful parting
as the last farewell.
See how the land runs,
the trees say goodbye shaking their leaves
while I re-make myself elsewhere thinking
about the woods, the stubbled fields.

1942

Solitaria natura

I

Solitaria natura
quando le spighe d'oro
cullano frusciando
il sogno dell'Estate;
che il tempo rallenta il suo turno
incede con battiti e tonfi
tra pause incalcolabili.
L'evento è il sordo fulmine del sole.
Le vigne verdi soltanto resistono:
ribollirà nei tini l'uva rossa.

II

Solitaria natura
stupiscono fanciulli
cui riescono pupazzi
d'argilla nelle cave,
germogli crescono
nel vento, nell'ombra.
Su mio padre steso nella terra
nasce un tappeto di dalie.
Il cimitero è il solo
giardino del paese.

1942-3

Solitary Nature

I

Solitary nature
when golden ears of corn
rustling sway
summer's dream
and time's motion slows,
advancing in fits and starts
and countless pauses.
The sun's deaf thunderbolt has struck.
Only green vines survive:
red grapes will lie fermenting in their vats.

II

Solitary nature.
Children amaze us
with puppets they have moulded
out of quarried clay,
shoots sprout up
in wind and shadow.
Over my father laid in the ground
a carpet of dahlias is blooming.
The only garden in the village
is the graveyard.

1942-3

Mitologia

Venivo alzando un tempio alla mia vita,
ove fossero quadri di Nostalgia
e di Dolore
di tutte le Finzioni che fermai
chinando il capo sulla terra
sotto il sole.
Sassi e mezzi limoni spremuti,
arsi sulla corteccia,
cocci di vasi di vetro
di ceramica e di terracotta,
legavano gli occhi in una nube
da cui fissare una loro leggenda.
Ebbi Terrore: che le cose sparse
e senza nome
tenessero linguaggi sovrumani!
E qualche coccio riluceva bianco
certo del suo segreto.

Tricarico, febbraio 1943

Mythology

I had been raising a temple to my life
hung with paintings of Nostalgia
and of Pain
and of all Untruths and so I stopped
and bowed my head to the ground
under the sun.
Stones and half-lemons squeezed dry,
their peels burnt,
shards of vases of glass,
ceramic and terracotta,
bound my eyes in a cloud
from which to gaze upon their story.
Terror seized me: that scattered
nameless things
should possess tongues beyond the human!
And one among the shards gleamed white,
sure of its secret.

Tricarico, February 1943

E nel cervello straripa

Dal mio mondo decimato
quando vago stormire di vento
volge faccia alle foglie
in annuncio di rondini bianconere,
rivolgo passi e pensiero
e cruda una voce mi strappa:
Bisogna andare, bisogna partire.
Sulle mie orme
batte il mio nome il cuore della mamma:
Ritornare, figlio, ritornare.
E nel cervello straripa
l'orologio delle ore incantate:
Più in là, più in là quel porto
dove ancora non so.

marzo 1943

And in My Mind....

As I wander away
from my wrecked world
the rustling wind
turns the face of the leaves,
heralding the black and white swallows.
I retrace my steps and thoughts
and a rough voice pulls me up:
You have to go, you have to go away.
My name, my mother's heart,
beats in my footsteps:
Come back, son, come back.
And in my mind the clock
overflows with enchanted hours.
Further on, further on lies that harbour.
I still don't know where.

March 1943

Banditore

Mi scalda tanto il sole
tra bianche nubi in corso.

Vengo al di là di queste terre
che oscillano come foglie al fuoco,
muti paesaggi ho travalicato
e c'è un coro di galli
nelle grotte del paese conchiglia.

Si spandono i dolori riasciugati
sono le nostre passeggiate eterne
verso giorni dimenticati.

E il banditore che soffoca i suoi gridi
tra le case dissotterrate racconta
del nostro andare inesorabile
verso il tramonto.

marzo 1943

Auctioneer

How badly the sun burns me
through the passing white clouds.

I come from beyond these lands
oscillating like leaves in a fire.
Across silent landscapes I have come
and a chorus of cocks is crowing
in the caves of the village shaped like a shell.

Sorrow's tears are spilled and dried again,
they are our endless paths
back to forgotten days.

And the auctioneer whose cries are muffled
among houses hollowed from the earth
tells of our inexorable path
into the sunset.

March 1943

Messa a 'Lo Spirito Santo'

Un odore di catacomba
'Preghiamo'.
Sulle pareti
rose dall'umido
o pure dall'abbandono,
umili barbagli.
Allegri della voce
del prete ridestata:
'Preghiamo o Fratelli'.
Il tonfo del petto d'una vecchia
accoccolata nelle vesti:
'Santo, Santo, Santo'.
Echi smorti della strada,
l'attesa delle panche vuote
e d'un ritratto spiritato,
la fresca terra baciata:
'No, Signore, io non son degno!'
tre volte
ed il silenzio lungo.
'Dilanio, Signore, le tue carni,
il tuo sangue mi bevo.
Per ogni secolo nei secoli
su questo crudo altare noi ti abbiamo
nuovamente ucciso, Signore'.

octobre 1943

Mass to 'The Holy Spirit'

Scent of catacombs
'Let us pray'.
On the walls
pink from the damp
or even from neglect,
humble flickers of light.
Allegri from the re-awakened
voice of the priest:
'Let us pray, O Brothers!'
Huddled inside her clothes, an old woman
thumping on her chest:
'Holy, holy, holy'.
Faint echoes from the street,
the waiting for empty pews,
a portrait possessed of the spirit,
the cool ground kissed:
'No, Lord, I am not worthy!'
Three times
and the long silence.
'Lord, I tear your flesh,
I drink of your blood.
Throughout the ages
we have on this crude altar
slain you anew, Lord.'

October 1943

Sera potentina

Sera potentina
con uno sbuffo di treno
e qualche imperlatura sulle colline,
me ne vado.
Il ponte di Monreale
ritto con otto luci
qui negli occhi.
La giostra di Via Pretoria
dopo giri più lenti s'è fermata
e tutto è maceria
di cose bombardate,
crepacci di bombe
e fili penzoloni.
Ma l'ombra c'inganna
la tarda memoria.

1943

Potenza Evening

Potenza evening
with a puff of the train
and some beading of pearls on the hills,
I am leaving.
The Monreale bridge
stands high with its eight lights
here in my eyes.
Via Pretoria's carousel
after ever slower turns has stopped
and everywhere are ruins
of bombed-out things,
bomb craters
and wires dangling.
Shadows, though, deceive us,
memory lingering.

1943

Cantico

Proprio che brillava la terra
quel mattino di primavera.
Il verde latteo dei seminati
occhieggiava tra le porche
e i sentieri e le rupi
erano di bianco immacolato
come le cascate di altri paesi.
Di là, mirando Ponente
piccoli colli in fila
su piano ondeggiante
formavano in grande
un palcoscenico illuminato
dove sarebbe tramontato.

Incanto di vita nel suburbio:
la capra pregna è menata al prato
dal garzone come a una passeggiata.
L'erbetta aggrappata sui margini
dorme tiepido sonno.
La gallina scava una fossa per dormire,
assaggia escrementi
e ripulisce il becco ad una pietra.
I fanciulli fanno piccole case col terriccio,
o giocano a gruppetti di non più di quattro
la loro favola bella.
Qualche adulto aduggiato sotto un portico
assolato non sa che fare.
La biancheria si svolge sulle pietre della torre.
Rifulge il ferro d'una zappa
come nella cantinella si rispecchia il sole.
Infanzia di tutti i tempi
con sbadigli e riflessi
concepita senza peccati.
Il camino è solitario del tetto.
Né sa la massaia che accende il focolare
né vede come il camino
fuma lento il sereno del cielo.

1943

Canticle

How the land shone
that spring morning.
The milky green of the sown fields
peeped over the ridges,
and the paths and the rocks
were an immaculate white
like the waterfalls in other countries.
From there, looking towards the West,
little hills in line
on an undulating plain
were, on a large scale,
setting up a stage with lights
where the sun would set.

The charm of life on the outskirts of town:
the pregnant goat is led to the meadow
by the goatherd as if off for a walk.
Grasses clinging to the edges
droop and doze.
The hen scrapes a hole to sleep in,
pecks droppings
and cleans her beak again on a stone.
Children build little houses with the soil
or, in groups of not more than four,
act out their fabulous tales.
An adult shadowed in a sunny porch
does not know what to do.
The laundry is spread on the stones by the tower.
The iron of the hoe glints
as sunlight is reflected in the cellar.
Childhood of all ages,
yawning and instinctive,
conceived without sin.
The chimney on the roof is all alone.
The housewife lighting the fire does not know
nor does she see how the chimney
is slowly darkening the cloudless sky.

1943

Giovani come te

Quanti ne fissi negli occhi
superbi della strada, erranti
giovani come te.
Non hanno in ogni tasca
che mozziconi neri
di sigarette raccattate.
Non sanno che sperdersi
davanti alle lucide vetrine
alle dicende dei bar
ai tram in rapida corsa
alla pubblicità
padrona delle piazze.
Tanto perché il tempo si ammazzi
cantano una qualsiasi canzone,
in cui si chiamano fuorviati, si dicono
amanti del bassifondo
e si ripagano di comprensione.
Una canzone è per covare insano amore
contro le ragazze cioccolato
che sono un po' le stelle sempre vive
che sono la speranza
d'una vita sorpresa in un sorriso.

E quanti, ma quanti
vorrebbero la luna nel pozzo
una loro strada sicura
che non si rompa tuttora nei bivii.
Quando compiono un gesto il solo gesto
son lì coi mietitori
addormentati ai monumenti
che aspettano la mano sulla spalla
del datore di lavoro.
Sono coi facchini di porto
contenti della faccia sporca
e le braccia penzoloni
dopo che il peso è rovesciato.

Young Just Like You

How many of them you stare at,
a street-wise look in their eyes,
drifters, and young just like you.
With nothing in their pockets
but the blackened stubs
of scavenged cigarettes,
all they know is how to lose themselves
in sparkling shop windows,
at the entrances of bars,
by the speeding trams,
or the publicity hoardings
that own the city squares.
Only to kill time
they'll sing some song
where they call themselves outsiders,
slum lovers,
and they are loyal to each other.
While in another song they'll nurse an unhealthy passion
for the black girls
who a bit like stars are always alive,
who offer the hope
of an unexpected life in a smile.

And how many, how very many of them
wish for the moon at the bottom of the well,
a path of their own, one that is safe
and will not always break up into other paths.
When they make a move, their only move,
they're at the side of the reapers
sleeping by the monuments,
waiting for a hand on their shoulder
from the man with an offer of work.
They're by the harbour porters
happy with their dirty faces
and their dangling arms
after they have dropped their burdens.

Son sprofondati talvolta in salotti
a far orgia di fumo e d'esistenzialismo
giovani malati come te di niente.

Spiriti pronti a tutte le chiamate
angeli maledetti
coscritti e vagabondi,
compagni dei cani randagi,
la nostra è la più sporca bandiera
la nostra giovinezza è
il più crudo dei tormenti.
Or quando la terra accaldata
ci mette addosso la smania del fuoco
nei lunghi meriggi d'estate,
è tempo di crucciarsi
di dir di sì all'Uomo che saremo
e che ci aspetta
alla Cantonata
con falce e libro in mano!

Napoli, giugno 1946

Sometimes they'll lounge around together
orgying on smoke and existentialism,
young and like you sick from nothingness.

Souls ready to respond to any call,
cursed angels
conscripted and wandering,
companions to stray dogs,
ours is the filthiest banner,
the period of our youth
the crudest of torments.
Now in the long summer noons
when the scorched land
turns us as restless as fire,
it is the time to cross ourselves,
to say yes to the Man we will become
and who waits for us
on the Corner,
sickle and book in his hand!

Naples, June 1946

Sera lontana

Batte già il mulo il ferro sopra il ciotolo
mentre si assestano i guanciali
nelle bisacce. Si parte così
nel Sud per le campagne la mattina,
per la stazione rossa sull'arena
del fiume, ogni anno mi parto anch'io.
Io non so se posso per il mondo
tenere il pugno chiuso nell'attesa
di sgranarlo nel giuoco della morra,
di tracannare oltre il desiderio
e sentire la lama del coltello
più calda della fetta rovesciata
sul tavolo a boccone dei compagni.
Di certo non potrò sentire i canti
le nenie della mamma e le assonnate
tiritere con zampogna e tamburino.
E....La stazione non è già montagna.
Tu non risali sull'imbrunire
con frutti acerbi, paglia e fiasco vuoto
non rivedi le quattro luci a segno
di tutto il lungo borgo addormentato.
Han perduto sapore, spaesato
le tue parole. La tua terra, cara
terra, che lì questa notte respira
con grilli ridestati e le stelle,
passa qui per un inutile inferno.

Tricarico, settembre 1946

Distant Evening

Already the mule's iron hoof is striking the cobblestones
as they fit their pillows into their saddlebags.
This is how they leave for the countryside
every morning in the South.
I leave each year too, for the red station
on the bank of the river.
I don't know if throughout my journey
I can keep my fist clenched, waiting
to open it for the game of *morra*,
to drink to excess
and to feel the blade of the knife
hotter than the slice fallen
on the table at a snack with friends.
It's certain that I will no longer hear the songs,
my mother's lullabies and drowsy rhymes
played on the *zampogna* and tambourine.
And....the station is no longer mountain.
You don't climb up at dusk
with unripe fruit, straw and empty flask,
nor do you see the four lights of the sleeping town.
Away from home, your words have lost
their flavour. Your land, your beloved
land, breathing over there tonight
with re-awakened crickets and the stars,
is suffering here a useless hell.

Tricarico, September 1946

Pasqua '47

In questo sole acceso sui torrenti
il bosco ci scintilla di primule e viole
e il vento ora fa suono tra le fronde
ora i pastori risoffiano le zampogne.
Oh quest'oggi gli uomini redenti
(c'è un treppiedi ricolmo
di tutti i cibi mancati dell'inverno)
ecco sanno baciarsi nelle strade
e di lontano riconoscersi fratelli.
Tu babbo di là dai pini che mi dici?
Non posso più baciarti la mano del sangue
né chiederti bene ginocchioni
ed averne due soldi nella giubba.
La bacio ai tuoi campagni ciabattini
ché so che sei contento.
Bevo oggi con loro che non hanno
vino, bastevole per dissetarsi.
E così vedo che risusciti anche te
con tutti i morti della terra
nel pianto della mamma
avanti il fumo del primo piatto.
E sento il dolore della miseria
dei servi ammessi ai tavoli
nelle case dei padroni, oggi.

Easter '47

The sun blazes above the streams,
the wood with its primroses and violets dazzles us
and now, as the wind rustles the leaves,
the shepherds play their reed-pipes again.
Oh today the redeemed men
(there's a three-legged stool piled high
with food they went without in winter)
embrace in the streets, and from across the way
recognise each other as brothers.
And you, father, there beyond the pines,
what can you say to me?
No longer can I kiss the hand of my blood
nor, on my knees, ask you for a treat
and get two pennies in my pocket.
So I kiss the hands of your fellow shoemakers
and know that it will please you.
Today, I drink with those who do not
have sufficient wine to slake their thirst.
And that is how I see you too
rise up with all earth's dead
in mother's weeping
as she sits before the first served
steaming dish.
And I feel the painful misery
of servants admitted to the tables
in the houses of their masters, on this day.

Le magiare attaccano la notte

Le magiare attaccano la notte
la nostra cavalla saura.
Si è trovata la criniera
annodata e non si divide più.
Serve di briglia a loro.
La troviamo sudata all'alba
le magiare la scelsero
in quella riunione che decise
la vita del nostro primo figlio.

1947

At Night the Witches Harness

At night the witches harness
our sorrel mare.
Her mane is now so knotted
that it will not part in two.
They use it as a rein.
At dawn we find her bathed in sweat.
The witches picked her out
that time they met
to decide our first son's life.

1947

Leggenda di amore

Donne che dormite
nella finestra di sole
che sboccia dal vicolo, mi dite
dove l'hanno reclusa la mia bella,
la furia abbandonava i focolari,
le piaceva di più la selce calda
cui s'addossava con le gambe lunghe?

-Ohi che sarà quella che lamenta
sotto la cuna a vento dei bambini!

O donne, quella se ne venne con me,
e fu docile all'erba,
alle onde respiro del mare.
Donne, accasava nei pioppi del pantano
e mi venne a cercare sulla montagna
dove spiccavano i fori delle carbonaie
nel campo nemico della notte.

-Ohi, solamente le lupe
si fanno i richiami tra i boschi e i pantani,
e le volpi si accecano ai fuochi,
e le civette sgridano la passione,
invano chiamano l'amore nelle notti!

Donne non maledite
la vostra insolita sorella
che prese dai padri arabi
il suo cuore pregno di sangue.
Lì, sulle sabbie che girano il mondo
sommosse dai venti africani,
per due fragili vite
rotte e riunite come due granelli,
amori uccisi perché amori maledetti,
carovane e uomini e donne amanti
accatastarono in faccia al mare
la pietra del pianto.

Legend of Love

Women sleeping
in the sun-filled window
that opens on the alleyway, tell me
where they have concealed my beautiful one:
the fury abandoned the hearth,
did she prefer the warm flint,
there to stretch her long legs?

Oh shame, it will be she who is grieving
under the children's cradle of wind!

O women, she came along with me,
she was docile in the grass
and in the waves, breath of the sea.
Women, she settled among the poplars in the marsh,
and on the mountain came to look for me
where the holes in the charcoal kilns,
night's enemy, glowed in the field.

Alas, only the wolves
call to one another from wood to marsh,
and the foxes are blinded in fires
and the owls are scolding passion,
in vain they call out for love through the nights.

Women, do not curse
your extraordinary sister
who took from her Arab parents
a full-blooded heart.
There, on sands circling the world
blown by African winds,
it was for two fragile lives
broken apart and joined again like two grains,
loves killed because they were loves cursed,
it was for them that caravans, men and women, lovers,
piled up the rock of tears
overlooking the sea.

Donne, ma dove l'hanno reclusa?
In cima ai tetti la sua voce di civetta non la sento.
Andiamo, venite nel vento africano
a scavare il suo cuore di polvere....

È il vento africano, soffia dal pantano,
regge le nuvole fosche sulle criniere dei boschi.
E io chiamo e canto, e inseguo quel vento.

1947-48

Where, women, where have they locked her away?
I cannot hear her owl's voice over the rooftops.
Come, let us go into the African wind
to excavate her heart of dust…

It is the African wind, blowing from the marsh
bearing dark clouds over the crest of the woods.
And I call out and sing and I follow that wind.

1947-48

Dormono sulle selci più grosse

Le ginestre delirano sui bordi
dei canali. E colombi e tordi
invano nelle ore risalgono
il cammino dell'acqua.
Battono il primo grano nel piazzale.
Un'altra sera e vi sarà nidiata
d'uomini distesi nell'aiata.

Così maggio è passato
un aereo nel cielo
che lo guardi fin che puoi
una fanciulla nel tenero velo
l'adolescenza scritta nel quaderno
un limbo, ora l'inferno.

Ora hanno trovato
le donne nello stipo
un serpente addormentato.
E i mietitori nelle giubbe rosse
cercano il letto sulle selci grosse.

1948

They Sleep on the Wide Stones

The broom thrashes madly on the banks
of the canals. And pigeons and thrushes
fly through the hours
upstream in vain.
On the square they are beating the first corn.
Another evening and there will be a nestful
of men stretched out on the threshing floor.

In this way May has passed,
a plane in the sky
that you look at as long as you can,
a young girl in a soft veil,
adolescence written down in a school book,
a limbo, now hell.

Now in the cabinet
the women have found
a sleeping serpent.
And the reapers in their red coats
look for a bed on the wide stones.

1948

Piove miele alle zitelle

Ai vetri tuoi sempre un tetto con muschio
un po' di pallido cielo e la costa
del monte ritoccata appena.
Se si potesse concedere il dono
il fondo dei tuoi occhi –
aspettano un muoversi di passi
là sulla rotabile che taglia
la cima della montagna! –
Quando più ardono gli arrivi
è all'alba e al tramonto
e i nostri gesti sono assai più vivi.
Ma quei passi lesti
ma dove li vedesti?
mica s'aprono al tuo davanzale
erano nel meriggio della sala
un trepidare d'ali di farfalle
al Cinema, ricordi.
E aspetti ancora al balcone maliardo
mosso dai tempi:
vi hai vissuto e sole e neve
eri una vampa nel recinto breve.
Tu solo puoi calcare le tue piste
infinite tra le quattro pareti
che so che ti ritrovi a quella vista
sempre, alta del tuo minareto.
Io vedo cangiare il tuo viso
nelle ore del giorno
quanto amore tu fingi
col sorriso disadorno.
E quale grazia vuoi
che ti porti la noia?
E chi passa chi guarda dalla strada?
Ti reclini nel vuoto disperata
il capo al fondo dei deliri antichi
e come piovono i serti dei fichi
il miele d'oro sulle tue pupille!

1948

Honey Rains on the Unmarried Women

From your window there is always a roof with moss,
a patch of pale sky and the mountain side
with its slight changes of shade.
If the depths of your eyes could just
give up their gift –
they wait for a movement of footsteps
there on the carriage road that cuts through
the mountain top! –
It is at dawn and sunset
that arrivals excite the most
and when our gestures are so much more alive.
But those light steps,
where did you see them?
They do not lead to your window ledge,
they were in the hall at noon,
a trembling of butterflies' wings
in the Cinema, you remember.
And still you wait at the charmed balcony
removed from the times;
there you lived and through sun and snow
you were a flame within your narrow confines.
Only you can pace your endless
walks within the four walls
but I know you always find yourself again
facing that view, from your minaret on high.
I see your face change
through the hours of the day
depending on how great the love you feign
with that plain smile.
What grace do you hope
this monotony might bring you?
And who passes by, who looks up from the street?
In the emptiness your head is bowed
in despair, lost in your old wild dreams,
and how the garlands of figs
rain golden honey on your eyes!

1948

Del lungomare in città

C'erano i lampioni in fila
del lungomare in città
e le sere
tarde un carrozzare lento del sonno
contavano le bottiglie vuote
chiudevano le bancarelle
e non sapevo se più amare i ladri
o le ragazze che vendono il corpo.
Che può fare il tuo sputo
nel mare veste di raso
che l'adornano le luci
viole e azzurre
delle leggende della città.

1948

Along the Seafront in the City

The street lamps stood in a line
along the seafront in the city
and in the late
evenings slowly a drowsiness crept in.
They would count the empty bottles,
the street stalls would close down
and I didn't know whom to love more, the thieves
or the girls who were selling their bodies.
What impression can your spittle make
on the satin dress of the sea
adorned with the violet and blue lights
of the legends of the city?

1948

Noi non ci bagneremo sulle spiagge

Noi non ci bagneremo sulle spiagge
a mietere andremo noi
e il sole ci cuocerà come la crosta del pane.
Abbiamo il collo duro, la faccia
di terra abbiamo e le braccia
di legna secca colore di mattoni.
Abbiamo i tozzi da mangiare
insaccati nelle maniche
delle giubbe ad armacollo.
Dormiamo sulle aie
attaccati alle cavezze dei muli.
Non sente la nostra carne
il moscerino che solletica
e succhia il nostro sangue.
Ognuno ha le ossa torte
non sogna di salire sulle donne
che dormono fresche nelle vesti corte.

1948

No Bathing at the Beaches for Us

No bathing at the beaches for us,
we're off to harvest
and the sun will bake us like a crust of bread.
We have tough necks, faces
of earth and we have arms
of dry, brick-coloured wood.
Our snacks are bundled
in the sleeves
of our jackets.
We sleep on threshing-floors
tied to the halters of our mules.
The midge that tickles
and sucks our blood
doesn't smell our flesh.
Not one of us with our twisted bones
dreams of mounting the women
who sleep, cool in their short dresses.

1948

Montescaglioso

Tutte queste foglie ch'erano verdi:
si fa sentire il vento delle foglie che si perdono
fondando i solchi a nuovo nella terra macinata.
Ogni solco ha un nome, vi è una foglia perenne
che rimonta sui rami di notte a primavera
a fare il giorno nuovo.
È caduto Novello sulla strada all'alba,
a quel punto si domina la campagna,
a quell'ora si è padroni del tempo che viene,
il mondo è vicino da Chicago a qui
sulla montagna scagliosa che pare una prua,
una vecchia prua emersa
che ha lungamente sfaldato le onde.
Cammina il paese tra le nubi, cammina
sulla strada dove un uomo si è piantato al timone,
dall'alba quando rimonta sui rami
la foglia perenne in primavera.

gennaio 1950

Montescaglioso

All these leaves that once were green:
the sound of leaves being shed is carried by the wind
that drives the furrows in the churned-up earth again.
Each furrow has a name, and there's a perennial leaf
which comes back on to the branch at night in spring
to make the day new.
Novello fell on the road at dawn,
at that point which overlooks the countryside,
at that hour when you rule the time to come.
From Chicago to here the world is near
on the scaly mountain that looks like the bow of a ship,
an old bow that has risen up
and for a long time smashed the waves.
The village walks through clouds, walks
along the road where a man has stood up at the helm,
at dawn when on the branch
the perennial leaf comes back in spring.

January 1950

La cantata a Monticchio

I monaci fratelli del silenzio
vennero ai due laghi occhi del cielo
che si sono posati sulla terra.

Occhi del cielo, occhi del cinghiale
aperti ai mille colori del sole.

Vulture e vento, gli alberi che danzano,
il fuoco spento è nella nuvola bianca,
Nuvola bianca dinne la vicenda:
'Son tanti anni alle carezze del vento...
ero nata in fondo all'Ionio una giumenta
e una giumenta al mare non può stare.
Austro vago di me, io timida di lui,
andava avanti e indietro aprendo i varchi
dei monti e s'appendeva alla mia chioma,
venne la sera, io mi volli fermare,
ci vedemmo specchiati in una fonte,
cresceva la luna reclina sui boschi,
di amore l'acqua si mise a cantare.'

I monaci fratelli del silenzio
li menò un solitario boscaiolo
che sapeva parlare col cinghiale.

Occhi del cielo, occhi del cinghiale
aperti ai mille colori del sole.

La nuvola bianca se n'è andata
sfumando la sua forma cavallina,
i monaci sepolti alle radici
e gli alberi cantano mattutino,
e l'acqua ricresce e canta e freme
per le fresche memorie
che noi saremo e per le belle storie.

1951-2

The Cantata at Monticchio

The monks brothers of silence
came to the two lakes eyes of the sky
that had settled on earth.

Eyes of the sky, eyes of the boar
open to the sun's thousand hues.

Vulture mountain and wind, dancing trees,
the spent fire is in the white cloud,
white cloud, tell us your story:
'For so many years caressed by the wind...
I was born a mare in the deep Ionian
and a mare cannot stay in the sea.
South wind, indistinct to me, I shy of him,
he went ahead and I following learned
the ways through the mountains, he hung on my mane,
evening came and I wanted to stop,
in a spring we saw our reflection,
over the woods the moon was waxing,
then the water sang of love.'

The monks brothers of silence
were led by a solitary woodman
who knew how to talk with boars.

Eyes of the sky, eyes of the boar
open to the sun's thousand hues.

The white cloud has gone,
its horse shape dissolved,
the monks in their graves at the roots
and the trees singing matins,
the water returns, singing and rippling
for the fresh memories
that we will become and the beautiful stories.

1951-2

È fatto giorno

Scegliere me la voglio la più bella
terra per terra la voglio portare
(da un canto popolare)

I

È fatto giorno, siamo entrati in giuoco anche noi
con le faccie e i panni che avevamo.
Vanno i più robusti zappatori
a legare il battaglio alle campane:
oggi deve bastare questo canto
dei cortei vagabondi
verso le piccole croci di legno.

È salita dalla Rabatana
è scesa dalle case del Monte
la folla dei pastrani
che macchiano le vie
e battono le mani.
Ma crudeli mostri di cartone
crescono sui loro capelli:
benedicono, gettano soldi
come confetti, e scuotono la frusta.

II

Esce allora uno scalzacane informe
che ha miracolosamente voce
dice lui di un luogo nascosto
e di una donna che dorme.

Sappiamo tutti la tua vera gloria
Signore della Croce
che non hai più bisogno d'incensi.

It's Light Now

Choosing, I want the most beautiful one,
carrying her from one land to another
(from a popular song)

I

It's light now. We too are playing our part
with the faces and the clothes we used to wear.
The heftiest hoers go
to tie the clappers to the bells:
today this song must suffice,
sung by the processions filing
towards the little wooden crosses.

Out of the Rabatana
and down from the houses of Il Monte
has come the mantled crowd
staining the streets
and clapping their hands.
But cruel cardboard monsters
are growing from their hair:
they utter blessings, scatter coins
like sweets, and crack their whips.

II

Then here comes a misshapen vagrant
who has miraculously a voice.
He speaks of a hidden place
and of a woman who sleeps.

We all know your true glory
Lord of the Cross.
You have no more need of incense.

E voi risentirete un canto nuovo
che è il più antico gemito di un fanciullo
il più pazzo strillo di una donna.

E voi imparerete la via sottomessa
che viene da un paese dove bisogna andare
con la felicità della paura
di andare incontro all'amore.

III

Allungate i passi, papi e governanti
alla luce degli scalzacani che vi hanno smentito.
Perché nel cielo si alza il sole
e dice tutte le verità, anche di voi,
che per farvi accettare
ci togliete il cuore e la lingua.
Dice che due tizzoni fanno il fuoco
stasera nelle casupole affumicate.

IV

Aiuta, vento, lo scalzacane,
toccato dal filo del dolce sonno di lei,
che corre inseguito al suo scialle di rosa del tramonto.

Ella promette alla noia avvincente
la leggenda perduta
e che la notte non sarà più scura e silenziosa.

1952

And you will hear again a new song:
the most ancient wail from a young boy,
a woman's most demented scream.

And you will learn the path of humility
that comes from a village you must go to
in the happy trepidation
of encountering love.

III

Lengthen your stride, popes and governors, step into the light
of the vagrants who have denied you.
For the sun is rising
which speaks every truth, including yours,
and to accept it
you must rip out your hearts and tongues.
It says that two embers make the fire
this evening in the smoky cottages.

IV

Wind, help the vagrant
who, touched by a thread of her sweet sleep,
chases the rose-coloured shawl of the sunset.

She promises against enthralling tedium
the lost legend
and a night no longer dark and silent.

1952